Emotional Freedom

Emotional
Freedom

Dr. Mario Rivera
Mendez

New Leaf Press

First Edition
1992

Library of Congress Catalog Number: 92-81732
ISBN: 0-89221-225-X

The English edition is translated by Dr. Elizabeth Harding, who specializes in counseling the dying. She is married with two young children.

Contents

Introduction

It may come as a shock to you when I say that you do not **have** problems. **YOU are the problem!** Indeed, unless you learn to live with yourself and enjoy your own company, your search for happiness will inevitably fail.

At the start, it is essential for you to know the answer to the question, "Who am I?" Only when you are able to attain a deep positive understanding of yourself, will you be able to enjoy being alone without the feeling of loneliness.

The German theologian, Dietrich Bonhoeffer, faced these questions and expressed his feelings in the following poem:

WHO AM I?

Who am I? They often tell me
I would step from my cell's confinement
calmly, cheerfully, firmly,
like a squire from his country-house.
Who am I? They often tell me
I would talk to my warders
freely and friendly and clearly,
as though it were mine to command.

Who am I? They also tell me
I would bear the days of misfortune
equably, smilingly, proudly,
like one accustomed to win.

Am I really all that which other men tell
of? Or am I only what I myself know of
myself? Restless and longing and sick,
like a bird in a cage, struggling for
breath, as though hands were
compressing my throat, yearning for
colours, for flowers, for the voices of
birds, thirsting for words of kindness,
for neighbourliness, trembling with
anger at despotisms and petty
humiliation, tossing in expectation of
great events, powerlessly trembling for
friends at an infinite distance, weary and
empty at praying, at thinking, at
making, faint, and ready to say farewell
to it all?

Who am I? This or the other?
Am I one person today and tomorrow
another? Am I both at once? A hypocrite
before others, and before myself a
contemptibly woebegone weakling?
Or is something within me still like a
beaten army, fleeing in disorder from
victory already achieved?

Who am I? They mock me, these lonely questions of mine. Whoever I am, Thou knowest, O God, I am thine!

Letters and Papers from Prison
© S.C.M. Press

The aim of this book is to help you face up to yourself, find specific answers to these questions, and pinpoint areas of conflict in your life.

Ask yourself these questions:

Who am I?
What do I believe in?
Why do I feel the way I do?
What am I living for?

Once you have begun to discover your true self, you need to see that the "problem" is not the circumstances themselves but how your personality reacts to them. In order to deal with life's problems successfully, you need to see the difference between your reactions and your feelings so that you are not dominated by your feelings.

The natural tendency in all of us is to do the opposite. For example, when you react favorably, you decide that the circumstances are good. On the other hand, when you react badly, you decide that they are adverse. Because we react without thinking, our attention gets drawn away from the true problem.

The real problem is not the circumstances, it is

ourselves. We must learn to separate circumstances from feelings.

The purpose of this book is to help you to do precisely that.

You will need to start by realizing there is a difference between:

- that which actually **is** and that which you **believe** to be
- what **you are** and **what others say you are.**
- what the Bible actually says and what you **think** it says
- **knowing** God and knowing **about** God
- **trusting** God and your own **relationship** with God
- **being** a child and **acting** like a child
- **being** alone and **feeling** alone.

Consider a rainy day in summer. The vacationer is disappointed, whereas the gardener is pleased. The day is the same, but the attitude makes all the difference! By getting a true perspective, you will find your attitude changing and, as a result, your ability to face problem areas will improve.

As we study the life of Jesus, it becomes significant that He never reacted but always acted with complete authority in every situation. Circumstances never dictated what He felt nor did they determine His motives or state of mind.

For example, at the marriage in Cana, Jesus was fully in control while everyone else reacted to the circumstances. On the cross, He declared finished all that He had come to accomplish. He was able to say, "Father, into Your hands I commit My spirit."

The Lord Jesus acted with authority. He had authority. He knew who He was. Circumstances did not dominate Him in the slightest.

You, too, can have victory over your circumstances if you use your understanding of yourself in the correct way, rather than reacting in the "natural" way.

What is Theotherapy?

Theotherapy is a method of counseling that combines psychological insight with biblical principles to achieve a whole personality. The author has used this method successfully for over twenty-five years as a pastor, psychologist, and educator, and counseled thousands of people in crisis.

As you read this book you will easily identify with the situations described. All of us have personally experienced some of these emotions: depression, anxiety, uncertainty, fear, and worry. Because these emotions are acquired in childhood, it is essential to learn that to be **as** a child is not actually to **be** a child.

If, as an adult, you still react with the feelings of a child within you, you will not be able to adapt successfully to the stresses of life. For example, you will not be able to face the frictions in marriage or really fully enjoy life. Acting as a child in adulthood prevents you from experiencing life to the full.

God's plan for you is not merely survival but a full, happy, satisfying, and abundant life. This will not only give you great joy but will also inspire others and impart joy to them. Theotherapy aims to make adults fully developed personalities while retaining the freshness and interest of a child. Jesus told the disciples, "Except ye . . . become as little children, ye shall not enter into the kingdom of heaven" (Matt. 18:3).

The strength of theotherapy is its ability to put this concept into practice. It is all too easy to be inspired by books and sermons without being instructed on how to establish good habits in practice. In other words it's the old problem of "Don't do as I do, do as I say."

The goal of theotherapy, however, is not only to tell a person what to do but also to give guidelines on how to do it. In addition, this book will tell you why you're unable to do it yourself.

You will discover the difference between:

- true repentance and feeling remorseful
- feeling angry and holding a grudge
- experiencing times of fear and being in an anxious state
- being content and **appearing** joyful
- having faith and being at the mercy of emotions

- accepting people or merely
  tolerating them
- helping others to live or merely
  living among other people.

It is quite possible that your life is going in a direction that is not the best for you. It may seem that you are choosing the best way because you do not see other alternatives.

On one occasion a man of about forty came to see me and said, "I have decided to end my life. I have it all worked out."

I asked him which of the two statements I should take notice of. That surprised him greatly. I then simply added, "I believe that suicide is one solution. But I have the true solution," and went on to explain.

The man listened intently. Many years have passed since then, and he now laughs at his "brilliant plan." This is what Proverbs means: "There is a way that seems right to a man, but in the end it leads to death" (Prov. 14:12;NIV).

Allow me to help you turn your life in a new direction that will undoubtedly bring you into emotional freedom. Consider the words of Jesus: "... I have come that they may have life, and have it to the full" (John 10:10;NIV).

Why merely exist when you can **live**?

1

Fundamentals of Theotherapy

You have the potential to become a successful human being. God has already given you everything you need to be able to handle the demands you will face in this life. He always gives you the capacity to overcome everything that is asked of you. You have it all in potential. In fact, everyone is born with this potential.

Your strengths or weaknesses, however, are determined by the interaction between your natural tendencies and your social conditioning. That means your genetic ability and the experiences of your formative years determine your strengths and weaknesses. In fact, the development of your potential depends greatly on your experiences in childhood.

In order to establish a balance between your

potential and the demands made upon you in life, you must come into a living relationship with your Creator.

Theotherapy brings together techniques from several different sources in a practical way to change your basic way of thinking from destructive thought patterns to sound positive biblical thinking.

By combining sound biblical truth and standard psychological principles of insight, theotherapy provides a method of resolving, in a relatively short period of time, any inner conflicts arising from life's demands. When these concepts are applied they result in effective and lasting changes, enabling you to love properly.

The result enables you to be continually happy and of sound mind by filling your days with the presence of the Living Lord.

Sound Theology Leads to a Sound Mind

This axiom should be included in the education of every minister in pastoral or psychological training. Every Christian leader, and indeed every Christian, would benefit enormously from understanding and applying this principle.

The heart of sound theology is, of course, the Lord Jesus himself. It is the indwelling presence of the Lord Jesus Christ that brings life and health.

When referring to sound theology I mean those fundamental biblical principles that override traditions and personal viewpoints and are based solely on what the Bible teaches, without adding or subtracting anything. It is this emphasis on the absolutes of God and a confidence in His Word, anointed by the Holy Spirit, that will transform your life and bring you peace.

The apostle Paul wrote, "For I determined not to know any thing among you, save Jesus Christ, and him crucified" (1 Cor. 2:2).

This principle of "sound theology/sound mind" is very important for your spiritual life and emotional well-being. I have found that many people experience a deep inner release, freedom from fear, guilt, anxiety, or whatever, at the moment they receive sound biblical truth. As they apply this truth in their heart they begin to free themselves from the bondages that held them captive. At that point, emotional and spiritual growth starts.

Who is Jesus Christ?

I was asked one day by a fifteen-year-old boy, "If Jesus is God, then what happened to the world when it was left without God when Jesus died?" This may seem an ingenious question to theologians, but what this boy was really asking, and what many people are confused about, is "Who really is Jesus Christ?"

It is very important to know who Jesus is, not just who we perceive Him to be. Was He man or God? To answer the young man's question we need to look at the Scriptures.

First, **God is one:**

> This is what the Lord says — Israel's King and Redeemer, the Lord Almighty: I am the first and I am the last; apart from me there is no God (Isa. 44:6;NIV).

What is God's name?

> Who has gone up to heaven and come down? Who has gathered up the wind in the hollow of his hands? Who has wrapped up the waters in his cloak? Who has established all the ends of the earth? What is the name, and the name of his son? Tell me if you know! (Prov. 30:4;NIV).

What is the name of God's Son?

> And a voice came from heaven: "You are my Son, whom I love; with you I am well pleased" (Mark 1:11;NIV).

It is obvious from this passage that His name is the Lord Jesus Christ. Jesus is identified by God himself as the One we must obey.

> While he [Peter] was still speaking, a bright cloud enveloped them, and a voice from the cloud said, "This is my Son, whom I love; with him I am well pleased. Listen to Him!" (Matt. 17:5;NIV).

The Lord Jesus, the Son of God, is God.

In the beginning was the Word, and the Word was with God, and the Word was God (John 1:1;NIV).

The Word became flesh and lived for a while among us. We have seen his glory, the glory of the one and only Son, who came from the Father, full of grace and truth (John 1:14;NIV).

It is evident from the Bible that Jesus is the only begotten Son of God the Father, and that He is, therefore, God incarnate in human form. This truth, however, will cause some to argue that when Jesus died as a man, God died as well.

Looking at this more carefully, we see that Jesus had a double nature, being at the same time wholly man and wholly God. As a man He had a human mother, Mary, but no human father. Joseph was only His step-father since Jesus was conceived by the Holy Spirit. As God, Jesus had His Father in heaven but no mother. This is why He could say on the cross "Father, forgive them; for they know not what they do" (Luke 23:34).

When Jesus died on the cross, His humanity died. Jesus, as the only begotten Son of God, became man, so that the sons of men could become sons of God.

The Holy Spirit

The Holy Spirit is also God. The Trinity can be illustrated with the following diagram:

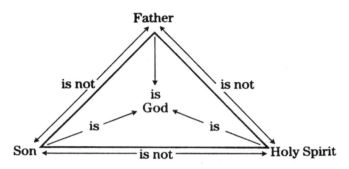

The triangle represents God. At each angle is one aspect of God. All are the same substance but distinct in the same way that the chemical substance H_2O, water, has three distinct states — gas, liquid, and solid. All are the same substance but are at the same time distinct in nature.

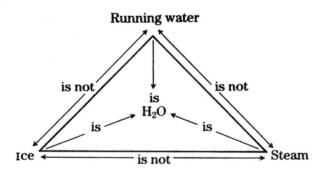

In the same way that God is three in one, mankind created in His image is also a being with the constituent parts — spirit, soul, and body.

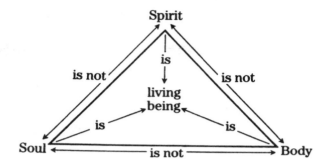

This basic principle used in theotherapy is grounded in the following Scripture:

> May God himself, the God of peace, sanctify you through and through. May your whole spirit, soul and body be kept blameless at the coming of our Lord Jesus Christ (1 Thess. 5:23;NIV).

Note the biblical order. The spirit comes first not the soul. This is important because it infers that God's intention is that the spiritual should reign over the psychological and the physical. The total composition of man is in these three parts. We must, therefore, start with this principle.

Basic Theological Concepts

1. Faith.

Faith overcomes the basic doubts of mankind. When you apply faith, it gives you vision and a goal to aim for. Faith also converges all your thoughts toward a single point of reference; that is to Christ. Faith directed in this way produces startling results with the minimum of effort.

Your faith has to be founded on what God has said, but that is exactly what makes it so effective.

The first step to active faith is receiving Christ into your heart and life as the One who always cares for you and has your best interests at heart.

2. Love.

All of us have a constant need to be loved. When you know that you are loved, you will be able to live feeling secure in your humanity. God is one of many who will love you. Indeed, when you, as a mere man or woman, discover that you were loved by God from even before the foundation of the world, and that God loves you as you are, you will come to accept yourself. Once you know you can love yourself and be loved, your self-esteem and self-knowledge will greatly improve.

The heart of theotherapy is love: giving out love and being a loving person. True agape love

- desires to give without asking for itself,
- always frees the one who is loved,
- accepts even when confronting at the same time.

You cannot have mental and emotional health unless you can both give love and receive it.

3. Truth.

Love in itself never sets men free. Only the truth actually sets you free.

Love gives security. Truth liberates.

Love covers. Truth confronts.

Love ensures that truth operates in balance.

Speaking the truth in love will bring a person to the critical point where they have to make a decision. Then they can be led on to forgiveness.

4. Forgiveness.

When you exercise faith, you begin to receive love. Love will lead you to truth, and love and truth working together will bring you to the point of experiencing forgiveness.

Forgiveness is not an emotion, but it is an act of the will entirely under your voluntary control. When you decide to forgive, you are not wallowing in sentiment but actually using your reason. Accepting the love of God for yourself and the accompanying forgiveness will lead you to forgive others. You can now truly forgive because you have been forgiven by God. You are able to forgive with the same forgiveness you have received.

Forgiving is not excusing or justifying. It is remitting the fault without allowing for circumstances. It is canceling the debt simply by a voluntary decision to do so. In other words, forgiveness is deciding to set the blame aside.

Jesus said, "And when you stand praying, if you hold anything against anyone, forgive him, so that your Father in heaven may forgive you your sins" (Mark 11:25;NIV).

5. Security of salvation.

Theotherapy creates a favorable atmosphere for a genuine, personal encounter with Jesus Christ. From your eternal security in Him will flow total mental health, rescuing you from the effects of your basic insecurities, lack of love, low self-esteem, and self-criticism. It will free you from the bitterness and resentment caused by the lack of forgiveness and, above all, allow you to be human and full of tenderness.

You will feel of value and be valued by others. Your life will have meaning because God loves you, forgives you, and accepts you. Christ confirmed that on the cross.

Your salvation is for all eternity, having been ratified on the cross and received at the moment of your conversion. Your salvation cannot be recalled, as the apostle Paul wrote, "For God's gifts and his call are irrevocable" (Rom. 11:29;NIV).

If you have this basic security, then total health will surely follow. After spiritual security, emotional and physical health are the end result.

What is faith?

Faith is having certainty in hope and having conviction without seeing. As the author of the Book of Hebrews wrote, "Now faith is the substance of things hoped for, the evidence of things not seen" (Heb. 11:1).

Faith is a gift of God for all who believe this truth.

> For it is by grace you have been saved, through faith — and this not from yourselves, it is the gift of God (Eph. 2:8;NIV).

How do you get this kind of faith? By asking!

> If any of you lacks wisdom, he should ask God, who gives generously to all without finding fault, and it will be given to him. But when he asks, he must believe and not doubt . . . (James 1:5-6).

God wants you to have faith. In fact, He will give it to anyone humble enough to ask for it. Even the twelve apostles said to Jesus, ". . . Increase our faith!" (Luke 17:5).

Faith is not an emotion; it is always based on testimony. The origin and source of faith is the Word of God itself.

> So then faith cometh by hearing, and hearing by the word of God (Rom. 10:17).

Faith based on experience alone is an insecure faith. The faith based on the Lord Jesus Christ — on who He is and what He has done — is always forceful and vigorous. Those who have this kind of faith will change nations and influence the world.

Emotional Addiction

When you realize that true, Bible-based faith is not an emotion but a deep conviction, do not assume you must exclude all emotion. On the contrary, true faith will always bring joy, hope, and peace. This faith is not based on, nor depends on, our own feelings but must be founded solely on who God is and His Word. This can be rather confusing for those who have to "feel" to believe, but a little patience and reading of the Gospel of John will help to change this attitude.

An undue dependence on emotions can produce an addiction similar to that of a drug addict. Emotional addiction, which is a dependence on emotions to be able to function adequately, destroys character and discourages spiritual maturity.

In fact, the exaggerated dependence on emotions is none other than the "child" inside demanding to be satisfied. The adult does not need to be satisfied in this way to do what needs to be done. Having to "feel" is nothing less than a rationalization of our sinful human nature in order to have faith.

Our carnal nature (the old sin nature, the old man) wants to control God. Anyone who allows his natural desires to control his relationship with the Lord can have "mystical experiences," but he must still be changed by the dealings of God in his life in order to become mature.

Jesus answered and said unto him, "If

a man love me, he will keep my words . . ."
(John 14:23).

This verse does not speak of feeling, for feeling is not enough. Faith based purely on emotions is very shaky faith. Emotional dependence does not help us cope with conflict adequately as Christians nor does it help us to worship God in a mature way.

Balancing Reason and Emotion

The opposite of emotional dependence is knowledge. But even knowledge on its own will not completely satisfy you either. An intellectual understanding that simply accepts the things of God through analysis and reasoning devoid of emotion will produce a cold person who lacks spiritual vitality.

The marriage of emotion and reason creates an even balance that produces joy and well-being. You need more than reason alone. You need not only to feel but to feel with reason or to reason with feeling. Let me give a parallel of this fusion.

Sodium (Na) by itself is a very reactive substance. Likewise, chlorine (Cl) on its own is also extremely reactive. When sodium and chlorine are combined to form salt (NaCl), however, the result is not at all reactive. The same can be said of hydrogen (H_2) and oxygen (O). Hydrogen is an explosive gas, and oxygen by itself is also highly dangerous and will produce an explosion at the slightest spark. The combination of the two, however, gives water (H_2O), which is not in the least explosive.

The combination of reason and emotion has the result of being neither reason nor emotion but rather faith.

Biblical Faith

To summarize the essentials regarding faith:

1. Biblical faith is not an emotion but a conviction.
2. Biblical faith does not depend on personal opinion but is based on the truth of the Bible.
3. The purpose of faith is primarily to equip us to confront our internal conflicts.
4. Faith is part of our character.
5. Faith equips us to worship, glorify, and serve God with humility of heart under all circumstances.

Most people ask for "faith" in order to resolve their inner conflicts or, to put it another way, in order to be better equipped to solve problems. If that were the purpose of faith, your problems would be overcome so fast that you would cease to need God. Then you would not need faith until the next problem came your way.

Faith, however, is not there to help you overcome your problems. It is there for you to use to adore, worship, and serve God.

When faith is used only to solve conflicts or to ask for our own petitions, we debase it to being a psychological tool. When this happens it corrodes our personality and sows the seed of unbelief.

Theotherapy deals with those things that inhibit the use of faith: problems, fears, anxieties, bad habits. These must be done away with.

You can heal yourself so that you do not have any hindrance to faith. This is important to grasp. Do not lose heart while resolving your inner conflicts because resolving them will allow your faith to flow freely without any hindrance toward the Lord.

Learn who God really is and that your faith should be directed toward adoring, worshipping, and serving Him. Give up the search for God's existence and start adoring and worshipping.

Effective Prayer

Many well intentioned people believe that when anyone has a problem all they have to do is pray. Of course, prayer is the best way to speak to God but, when the intention of the prayer is neurotic, it only serves to confirm people in their negative, non-biblical way of thinking. Let me illustrate.

After I had preached in a church one night, a young man full of fear came out to the front. He was sobbing and saying over and over again, "Lord, forgive me. Lord, forgive me. Lord, forgive me." He said nothing else but asked disconsolately over and over again. At first it didn't seem out of the ordinary that he had come to the altar, but after a while I could see that the more fearful requests he made the more it reinforced his sense of guilt.

God does forgive us. He accepts us and gives us His pardon. Often, however, we do not want to receive forgiveness because we wish to atone for our sense of guilt ourselves. Are you aware that this sentiment is totally contrary to biblical teaching? The Bible clearly states that "... the blood of Jesus Christ his Son cleanseth us from all sin" (1 John 1:7).

After I had finished speaking that night, the young man continued wrestling with his own feelings of guilt. I interrupted him and asked him to look into my eyes. When I could see that I had his attention, I asked him whether he thought God was deaf! Astonished, he said that he didn't think He was.

Then I continued, "I have heard you asking so many times for forgiveness, but you have not even begun to thank God for having forgiven you."

Greatly relieved, the young man thanked the Lord for being a forgiving God and for forgiving him. He immediately got up from his knees and went away with a smile on his face.

The truly effective way of praying is said in meekness and conforms only to the Word of God.

> ... You do not have, because you do not ask God. When you ask, you do not

receive, because you ask with wrong motives, that you may spend what you get on your pleasures (James 4:2-3;NIV).

When we use our prayers as a substitute for resolving our inner conflicts, then the words are totally empty. God will not respond to those who, as Jesus said, " . . . for a show make lengthy prayers . . ." (Luke 20:47).

Recently a lady who thought she was a Christian came to see me because she felt depressed and confused. She said that she prayed often and never missed church on Sunday. She also stated, "My mother was wonderful. She made sacrifices for me all her life. Now that she is dead, I am rewarding her by being devoted to prayer."

As she spoke, I noted she folded her arms, so I decided to confront her with her own attitude. Then, a bit sharply, I asked if she had anger toward her mother.

"I have no anger toward my mother. I am very religious and one could not have any anger toward such a proper mother as mine," she asserted.

I assured her that she could quite legitimately be angry, and that the Bible teaches that it is not a sin to have anger. The sin is keeping anger in our hearts and allowing it to become sin.

She said seriously, "Do you want me to tell you who I'm angry with? I'm angry with my father for not protecting me from my mother because she really didn't love me at all."

This woman now understood that all her life

she had used prayer as an excuse. As we got to the bottom of the problem, she began to resolve her inner conflict. Before leaving my office, she could pray and praise the Lord with hands uplifted. That's the kind of prayer that is always glorifying to God.

2

Seven Emotional Plagues

Almost everyone has heard of the four horses of the apocalypse of Revelation 6:1-8, but most people have little idea what they represent.

In Chapter 6 of the Book of Revelation, the four horses are described. The first one is white and refers to those whom God sent to travel up and down the land, probably as forerunners of the Lord. (See also Zech. 1:8-11.) The next horse in this passage is red — blood red — symbolizing the conflict of war and battle. The third is black and represents scarcity, need, or famine. The fourth horse is pale yellow, representing death.

Each of these symbols can create fear in man. However, God does not want you to have fear but joy and peace.

The Bible says that man can learn to live —

happy and cheerful — as God originally intended from creation. Still, in spite of God's plan, mankind has failed to solve not only the problems of famine, war, and death, but men have not even dealt with themselves and their modern "horses of the apocalypse."

What are these modern "horses of the apocalypse?" They are the emotional afflictions that plaque every man, woman, and child on the face of the earth.

Discouragement

Whenever you believe that you can achieve your goal, you run the risk of being discouraged. Several forces contribute to discouragement.

1. Discouragement is fueled by fear.

When you are in fear, you cannot achieve what you want to do. Fear is a powerful paralyzing agent that causes you to disarm yourself, leaving you defenseless.

Because God knew the children of Israel were afraid to go forward and take the land of Canaan from their enemies, He ordained Joshua as the social, political, and spiritual leader to encourage them. God says to you, as He said to Joshua: " . . . Be strong and courageous . . ." (Josh. 1:9;NIV).

Fear produces lack of faith in God, making you believe that you don't have the courage to achieve what you set out to do. This contributes still more to your lack of confidence.

For many Christians the use of the word "faith" is a way of excusing themselves. "If I had **enough** faith, then I could cope with all my problems."

When I hear this, I take it to mean, "If I only had confidence in myself," or, "If only I could believe that I am worth something." We need to learn how to distinguish between having faith in God and confidence in ourselves because one flows from the other.

Lack of self-confidence is really the reason many people are unable to put their trust in the Lord. Fear experienced in childhood will annihilate your self-confidence by subconsciously telling you that your faith in God is not to be trusted. This lack of confidence is often the reason we feel impotent and useless when faced with the stresses of life.

Let your faith in God be reasserted with the words of the Lord himself, "I am with you." Start to see things from a biblical viewpoint: God loves you, and He will give you the ability to love and serve Him.

2. The root cause of discouragement is actually fear of failure.

When you bring the experiences of past failure into the light, you begin to start conquering discouragement. Discover the cause of your inability to have the faith to succeed, and you will already be on the road to victory.

You can counter the offensive of discouragement with this verse: ". . . Not by might, nor by power, but by my Spirit, saith the Lord of hosts" (Zech. 4:6). You **can** do it because God has **said** that you can do it.

One day a young man came to see me and said he was faced with two problems. I assured him that he did not **have** these problems, but that **he** was his own problem. Rather disconcerted at this, the young man insisted that he really did have two very serious problems.

As I listened carefully to his story, I could see that he was on the brink of despair, which is why he had come to see me. His first "problem" was that he started each term at the university with great enthusiasm but before long lost all interest in his studies and began to fail his exams. The second "problem" was that all the girls avoided him. Here was a young man with a pleasant personality and good intelligence, yet in his personal relationships and studies discouragement had brought him to the point of failure.

When I asked him to share with me about his childhood, he replied that there had not been anything particularly terrible or even of note. So I asked him about his father.

"My father is a carpenter," he said and began to relate a significant incident. "One day when I was about eleven, I was helping him with his work. He shouted down at me from the roof of the house he was building, 'Hand me a wood chisel, quick!' By mistake I handed him a cold chisel. Immediately he shouted angrily, 'You'll never achieve anything in life. Clear off and don't offer to give me any help again.'"

The young man sat in silence. After a while I asked him how this made him feel. "I felt as I do now — worthless, good for nothing, incapable."

As we talked, he was able to see that the root cause of his discouragement and his fear of failure was directly related to this incident. Then he began to take heart.

I explained that he had to forgive his father as the Bible teaches, and that forgiveness was not an emotion but an act of his will. "Forgiving is something that must be done, not because you feel like it, but because God has ordained that it must be done," I told him.

The student was able to forgive his father and, more thrilling than that, to put his trust in God. The end result was that he subsequently made good grades in college and developed a steady relationship with a pretty girl!

You, too, can conquer your discouragement. Remember that God **in you** can do all things if you only put your trust in Him.

> May the God of peace ... equip you with everything good for doing his will, and may he work in us what is pleasing to him, through Jesus Christ ... (Heb. 13:20-21;NIV).

Guilt

The Lord Jesus Christ does not want to make

you, a sinner, feel continually guilty. In fact, to the woman caught in adultery Jesus said, ". . . Neither do I condemn thee: go, and sin no more" (John 8:11).

Guilt and condemnation never produce positive results because the consequences of guilt are always negative. The sense of guilt only leads to a feeling of remorse, and remorse is not repentance. When you feel loved, understood, and accepted, in spite of what you have done wrong, then you will find yourself able to experience true repentance.

It is important to distinguish between remorse and repentance because there is a big difference. Remorse is an internal weight that follows as the result of a wrong action. This feeling alone, however, does not bring correction, and its fruit is not all good. In this biblical example decide whether Judas experienced remorse or repentance:

> When Judas, who had betrayed him, saw that Jesus was condemned, he was seized with remorse and returned the thirty silver coins to the chief priests and the elders. "I have sinned," he said, "for I have betrayed innocent blood."
>
> "What is that to us?" they replied. "That's your responsibility."
>
> So Judas threw the money into the temple and left. Then he went away and hanged himself (Matt. 27:3-5;NIV).

The Living Bible says it this way, "Judas . . . changed his mind and deeply regretted what he had done." Judas experienced remorse but not true repentance.

Contrast Judas' experience with Peter's denial of Jesus:

> After a little while, those standing there went up to Peter and said, "Surely you are one of them, for your accent gives you away."
> Then he began to call down curses on himself and swore to them, "I don't know the man!"
> Immediately a rooster crowed. Then Peter remembered the word Jesus had spoken: "Before the rooster crows, you will disown me three times." And he went outside and wept bitterly (Matt. 26:73-75;NIV).

Repentance always enables you to achieve something as a result. Its end is always beneficial. Jesus said, "Produce fruit in keeping with" (Matt. 3:8).

Guilt tends to paralyze and produce fear. Sometimes we can even use it as a whip to chastise others or even ourselves. One of the games often played is to inflict a sense of guilt on other persons in order to manipulate them.

If your own relationship with God is good, and if you feel truly loved and accepted by Him, then you feel free. You will not have to use guilt to make others subject to your will, neither will you allow others to manipulate you in this way.

Guilt is one of two main types: existential or neurotic.

1. Existential guilt is experienced every time a sin is committed and is the direct consequence of a wrong action. If you don't do something you said you would, or you do something you know you shouldn't have done, you feel guilty.

The antidote to this kind of guilt is to confess your sin, accept your inability to change and your indebtedness to God, and hand the whole situation over to Him. Confession to the Lord and an acceptance of the responsibility for the sin by you is the cure for guilt.

You can then still love yourself while at the same time you are coming to grips with the problem. There is no sin that is so awful or big that the blood of Jesus cannot cleanse you from it.

2. Neurotic guilt is experienced internally, even though there is often an external expression.

For example, I know a lady whose mother died while giving birth to her. It seemed that others made the daughter feel, and she herself felt, that if she had not been conceived, then her mother would not have died.

"This is absurd," I told her, "because Scripture teaches that only God has the power to give life and only He has the power to take it, whether actively or permissively. Jesus said, '... Fear him [God] who, after the killing of the body, has power to throw you into hell. Yes, I tell you, fear him' (Luke 12:5;NIV). And the apostle Paul wrote, '. . . God, who gives life to everything . . .'" (1 Tim. 6:13;NIV).

Despite the woman's intellectual knowledge of these verses, she still felt responsible for her mother's death and was bound by a profound sense of guilt.

Finally, she was able to see her own sense of guilt for what it was and accept God's unconditional love and acceptance of herself. When she realized she was not responsible for her mother's death, she became perfectly free. Today she is a happy Christian who in turn brings joy to others.

Identify the true source of your own guilt and use the power of the Lord's forgiveness and acceptance to become free.

Anger

The problem with anger is that this emotion has several different ways of being expressed. Anger in itself is not a sin. To feel heated about an injustice done to you by someone else does not constitute a sin. Anger, however, becomes a debilitating scourge when it is not resolved properly. Anger turned inward can develop into more destructive sentiments.

Let us look at two of the various expressions of anger.

1. Resentment.

Resentment is simply latent anger that has not been dealt with satisfactorily. The person who bears a grudge becomes susceptible to illness, particularly arthritic or muscular problems and migraine headaches. He will also experience spiritual dryness.

The resentful person is not lovable and does not impart human warmth to others. Furthermore, the person's faith is maintained on the intellectual rather than the heart level. He may laugh with a mournful expression, full of feeling, but he doesn't often smile. A good smile reflects an attitude of acceptance and approval.

2. Hate.

In Ephesians 4:26 Paul writes, "Be ye angry, and sin not...." When anger moves from the head to the heart, it becomes hate, which most definitely is sin. Anger wishes to chastise; hate wishes to destroy and reveals itself in the desire to annihilate the victim. This is the heart of the situation.

Thoughts that are stirred up erupt into anger and cool off the instant they are expressed. Hate is always active, even if it is hidden for a while. The results of hate sooner or later rebound back on the hater like a boomerang. The real tragedy of hate is that it often results in self-hatred.

If you remember that **you** are your own problem and what you do is only partly related to your circumstances, then you will be able to deal with anger much more successfully than before.

Anger is a reaction to external stimuli. You should never let your circumstances determine your state of mind. In every circumstance exert your own authority over your feelings and do not allow them to become something destructive.

If you allow yourself to be filled with anger, you run the risk of it becoming resentment or even hatred. If, however, you decide to deal with your anger, you will liberate yourself and open yourself to receive from God the peace He wants to give you. The peace of God, however, cannot be manifested in a heart full of anger.

You need to know how to deal with your anger properly. The Bible has the answer in the second half of Ephesians 4:26: "Let not the sun go down upon your wrath." If you put this verse into practice, the psychological result is so profound that you would find real peace.

To keep yourself free of resentment and hatred learn to deal with your anger quickly and remember, "A gentle answer turns away wrath . . ." (Prov. 15:1;NIV).

Depression

Surprisingly, the word depression never appears in the Bible because the Jews had no word to describe this condition. The best definition is "sadness of heart," which defines depression as one of its symptoms.

Nehemiah's depression must have been evident because the king asked, ". . . Why does your face look so sad when you are not ill? This can be nothing but sadness of heart" (Neh. 2:2;NIV).

Depression is the dominant emotional ailment in our society. Nearly everyone has at some time or another become a victim of depression. Let us look at several causes of depression.

1. The home environment.

Intensive study has shown that children brought up in an environment with chronic depressive parents will suffer emotionally and physically. There is strong evidence that babies who are not talked to are retarded in their development and fail to learn how to communicate properly. Good psychological adjustment depends on a healthy environment in the formative years.

Consider the attitude of Jesus toward the disciples who wanted to stop the children in their laughing and playing: ". . . Let the little children come to me, and do not hinder them, for the kingdom of God belongs to such as these" (Luke 18:16;NIV).

The significant adults for most children are first of all their parents, the grownups he has most contact with. As the child grows, he will discover that he has grandparents, aunts and uncles, and teachers, all of whom have a significant place in his life.

Unfortunately, not everybody has a good psychological upbringing, which is why we need to cover this area.

2. Lack of satisfying personal relationships.

Every person needs satisfying relationships with other human beings, especially with those who are his "significant others." By this I mean all those on whose love and acceptance he depends for real self esteem: husband/wife, parent/child, employer/worker, etc.

In adult life, too, good relationships with others is also vitally important to maintaining a healthy outlook on life.

In my own life I have found that the relationship that is most satisfying and beautiful and brings me most satisfaction is my relationship with the Son of God. When the Lord Jesus Christ becomes a significant person in your life, you will discover a profound awareness of what life is all about. Everything will have meaning, as I discovered for myself.

Depression brings an emptiness to life and prevents the depressed person from establishing any deep relationships, particularly with a significant person in his life. The greater the number of "significant others" you can establish a deep, intimate bond with, the better able you will be to achieve good emotional adjustment.

When you have poor relationships with the significant adults in your life, you begin to feel lonely, and that has the effect of aggravating anger and guilt. That is why depression often accompanies these latter two conditions.

Before you can deal effectively with your feelings of depression, you must first deal with the anger, which is the result of not feeling loved and accepted. Then you must deal with the **guilt**, which makes you feel that you are to blame for being rejected.

Once you have resolved your guilt and anger and have been forgiven, then the invitation of the Lord Jesus is there to show you the way out of depression: "Come to me, all you who are weary and burdened, and I will give you rest" (Matt. 11:28;NIV).

There is also good reason to believe that where there is a good sense of social integration, a strong bond of love between family members and neighbors, and good permanent marriage relationships, then the physical health of the members of the family is improved and they tend to live longer.

The Bible has much to say about joy, which is the opposite of depression. One verse in particular is highly significant from a psychological point of view: ". . . the joy of the Lord is your strength" (Neh. 8:10;NIV).

This joy is not just cheerfulness, exuberance or superficial smiles, but an attitude of well-being that the Holy Spirit places in the hearts of those able to receive it. It is a permanent joy that is strong, vigorous, and resilient, and quite the opposite of depression, which saps energy and turns people into psychological and physical invalids.

It is possible to be continually joyful and, thus, to achieve stability in the depth of your heart. Confess all anger, all irritation, and also all guilt. Allow the Holy Spirit to lift you into His joy, the vibrant joy of God.

Fear

The first mention of fear in the Bible comes in Genesis 3:10 after Adam sinned and hid himself from God because he was afraid. In this verse you can see the logical conclusion of fear. Man is afraid of being discovered and of facing himself again afterward. Avoiding fear only created more fear.

What is fear? In the last analysis it is **pride.** Fear is not wanting to deal with your faults for fear that having uncovered them, others will consequently reject you.

Let me suggest two ways that will diffuse the fear in your life.

1. Accept God's unconditional love for you.

The basis of fear is the belief that you are not acceptable. As long as you determine that you are not loved, you will have fear. But if you accept God's unconditionally love for you, your fear and your pride will vanish. This is clearly seen in 1 John 4:18: "There is no fear in love; but perfect love casteth out fear . . . ."

God eagerly wants you to give Him your will in order to direct it toward himself. But even if you do not surrender your will to Him, He is still able to make you feel completely loved.

2. Accept your faults and be humble.

A meek person can allow himself to be loved and is free to love also. Meekness is not weakness nor is it the same as being afraid. Fear stems from a lack of humility.

If you learn to become meek and accept your faults, then the very people who condemned you before will find you irresistibly lovable!

Once you really grasp this truth and understand it, then you will no longer feel the need to hide — as Adam did. Instead, you will come to God in real humility, confess your failure, and know that you have no right ever to be afraid again.

You will know that God loves you.

Doubt

At a minister's fellowship meeting one day, a young Roman Catholic priest came to see me and confessed that he was often troubled by terrible doubts. As he spoke he lowered his voice, and I listened in silence for a while.

After a while he said, "This may surprise you, but I have even doubted the very existence of God himself." He fixed his eyes on me, searching for even the slightest hint of rejection in my expression.

He found none, and I answered him quite confidently to show that I had understood him correctly. "No, it doesn't surprise me."

After we had talked for a while, I was able to show him that doubt, when it is an honest questioning to find the truth, is not a sin in itself. "The apostle Thomas doubted," I explained, "but after-

ward was able to exclaim, 'My Lord and my God'"
(John 20:28).

This young priest had the boldness to acknowledge his doubts. Expressing them verbally
helped him to understand the deepest doubt in his
heart, which was really that he was not acceptable
to his parents. When he discovered how important he was to the Lord, he was then able to accept
and forgive his parents. At once his doubts evapo-
rated into thin air.

Doubts that are the result of a deep desire to
feel accepted are **neurotic doubts.** Far too many
Christians live with doubts that deny them the joy
of a loving relationship with their God. You need
to understand, right now, that your worth does
not depend on what you think of yourself. It
depends on what God has done for you. This is
what will enable you to resolve your inner conflicts successfully.

Let me give you another example. A nineteen-
year-old divorcee, the mother of a little girl, asked
me if it was possible to believe in God.

"Why not?" I answered.

"Well, one day my mother was drunk and had
intercourse with a man she had only just met. I was
the result."

I was able to help this young woman understand that we are born not just because of the
physical and biological process but because God
wants us to be born!

"Her worth and your worth do not depend at
all on the circumstances in which you were con-

ceived," I told her. "The Bible says, 'For you [God] created my inmost being; you knit me together in my mother's womb'" (Ps. 139:13;NIV).

After praising and thanking God for giving her life, this young woman went on her way rejoicing. As she left, she smiled and looked at me with pride, realizing that she was not just the chance happening of a human relationship but had been born as a product of the heart of God himself. Her original doubt had completely vanished.

Emptiness

How often we hear people saying "My life has no purpose, no meaning."

What they are really saying is that they feel they are no longer in control of their lives. In reality, life has **not** lost its meaning, but the feeling of emptiness is the result of their present circumstances. It's not necessarily the circumstances that need changed, however, it is the person himself who needs to change.

Even King Soloman, who was one of the richest men who ever lived, said:

"Meaningless! Meaningless!" says the Teacher. "Utterly meaningless! Everything is meaningless." (Eccles. 1:2).

When your life seems to have lost its purpose, ask yourself these questions: What, if I am really honest, do I want to do? Do I feel unable to face any part of my life?

One inescapable fact you cannot avoid is this: **Your personality has been created in such a manner as to find emptiness intolerable.**

Let me suggest two things you can do to fill the emptiness in your life.

1. Join a group of people who will support you.

The best "support group" is an active, Christ-centered church where your whole person can be ministered to — spirit, soul, and body.

In Puerto Rico, at the Barbara Ann Roessler Memorial Church, the needs of the individual and the needs of the community are taken care of at the same time. The church has been divided into "cells," or local area groups. These small community groups form the basis for providing the mutual support so vital to our emotional health.

I have written in more detail about how the church is structured in my book, *The Church as a Healing and Redemptive Community,* where I stress the need for a caring community to counteract the isolation so often experienced by twentieth-century man.

The human personality cannot cope within a vacuum. If you do not fill your days with values that give your life a purpose, you will find that other things sap life's meaning.

2. Give to others.

It is always in giving that you will find purpose in life. The Lord Jesus states this very clearly: "...It is more blessed to give than to receive" (Acts 20:35). Your life will take on a new meaning as you learn to give more.

The high divorce rate indicates mankind's need to find meaning in marriage. Many people think marriage is the relationship that will bring them happiness. This is not necessarily so.

Marriage is not a relationship where you should strive to achieve your own personal fulfillment, rather it is one in which you should be continually giving.

Giving is one of the main psychological characteristics of adulthood. The adult gives; the child demands. When anyone enters marriage with an attitude of asking to be made happy, he will not find happiness nor will he give it to others. This same truth affects all areas of life.

Your life will take on a new dimension and become more pleasing in proportion to your ability to give to others. That's the secret to finding meaning to being alive.

3

Six Truths That Will Change Your Life

After many years of counseling and pastoring, I have concluded that the Bible not only gives life to the spirit but also promotes good emotional health and even physical health.

"And ye shall know the truth, and the truth shall make you free" (John 8:32).

In order for you to experience emotional freedom, you have to know the Lord God as the author of the Bible. Let me restate unambiguously and directly that there is a world of difference between knowing **about** God and **knowing** Him personally.

In order for the healing power of the Bible to be effective it is essential for you to know God.

Man was created by God, and all his being is dependent on that intimate personal relationship with Him.

In order to have good emotional health, you do need to know yourself:

- your motives,
- your frustrations,
- your areas of rejection,
- your anxieties,
- your hopes,
- your faith.

In addition to knowing yourself, it is essential for you to know:

- why people have treated you the way they have,
- why that had the effect it did on you,
- how you can help **them** resolve their own conflicts.

How you see yourself, as well as how you see the answers to these questions, depends greatly on your perception of God. Without knowing Him, you will never know yourself fully or the full reasons behind the actions of others.

Attempting to answer all these questions by taking courses, reading books, or attending conferences will lead to an unfruitful search. Such activities may be very interesting and absorbing, but they will not, of themselves, bring healing.

Without the knowledge of God, you will never achieve total self-awareness.

Let me stress the point again. It is not **what** you know about God that counts, it is **knowing** Him.

In order to help you to know Him in a real and personal way, here are six things about God you need to know. These six truths can change your life.

1. God does not EXIST. He IS.

A final year chemistry student came to me one night with a question typical of a young mind: "If you can prove to me that God exists, then I'll believe in Him." In spite of his apparent skepticism, this young man did indicate a sincere desire to know God.

I remembered the conversation Jesus had with Nicodemus in John 3, so I asked the student to clarify exactly what he wanted. Did he want me to put God in a test tube and prove His existence, so that he could believe in Him?

As we talked I began to understand the intention of this brilliant student and said, "I can do better than that. I can introduce you to the Lord, and you can speak to Him yourself!"

I asked the boy to kneel with me right then and there in my office, and I put my hand on his head and prayed, "Lord, reveal Yourself to this young man because he wants to know You. Lord, make Yourself known to him for himself." Immediately, the young chemist started to weep.

Several years have now passed since that marvelous event, and today he is a preacher and master of the Word and is greatly used by God.

It is impossible to prove that God exists.

Anything that has been created can be proved. Certain intangibles, however, that exist eternally must simply be taken by faith. For example, the love of a young woman for a man cannot be proved. It must be taken on trust.

When a philosophy student was asked for a definition of love, the best he could do was: "Love is something you know when you love. Until you love you do not know what it is. I cannot explain it to you."

> Moses said to God, "Suppose I go to the Israelites and say to them, 'The God of your fathers has sent me to you,' and they ask me, 'What is his name?' Then what shall I tell them?"

> God said to Moses, "I am who I am. This is what you are to say to the Israelites: 'I AM has sent me to you'" (Exod. 3:13-14;NIV).

God is.

He has no beginning or end; He exists simply on His own, externally. Things that have been created exist; they have a beginning and an end. The Bible cannot define who God is because He has no beginning or end. It cannot give an empirical view of His existence. Scripture merely states: "In the beginning God . . ." (Gen. 1:1).

Jesus even refers to himself as, "I am the Alpha and Omega . . ." (Rev. 1:8; 21:6; 22:13). In other words, He is the A and the Z, the beginning and the end.

Because God is, you must approach Him in faith.

The Amplified Bible translates Hebrews 11:6 this way:

> For without faith it is impossible to please and be satisfactory to him. For whoever would come near to God must (necessarily) believe that God exists and that he is the Rewarder of those who diligently seek him.

Faith does not demand evidence, it just accepts.

Reason demands evidence of created things that exist. Faith accepts those things that are of themselves existent.

Often people confuse themselves unnecessarily because they fail to learn the fundamentals. Without a solid foundation you cannot build. Before understanding the complex, you must grasp the more simple. When you live in this way, faith will flow and a sense of well-being will become a reality.

The Bible speaks of Jesus, the Son of God, as a truth that does not need to be proved. Indeed, it does not even set out to prove that He is who He said He is.

And are built upon the foundation of
the apostles and prophets, Jesus Christ
himself being the chief corner stone; In
whom all the building fitly framed together groweth unto an holy temple in the
Lord (Eph. 2:20-21).

Suffice it to say that the Bible expounds what
is said concerning the Son of God.
Consider these passages:

For other foundation can no man lay
than that is laid, which is Jesus Christ (1
Cor. 3:11).
And did all drink the same spiritual
drink: for they drank of that spiritual Rock
that followed them: and that Rock was
Christ (1 Cor. 10:4).
Neither is there salvation in any other:
for there is none other name under heaven
given among men, whereby we must be
saved (Acts 4:12).

Nowhere will you find the Bible offering proof
of the existence of Jesus. It only reveals Him. He is,
and it is up to you to respond.

2. God does not LIKE you. He LOVES you.
I want you to understand that when I say that
God does not like you, I do not mean that He
dislikes you, but that His love goes way beyond
mere likes and dislikes. The Holy Spirit in you is

full of God's love. ". . . The spirit who dwelleth in us lusteth to envy" (James 4:5).

I want you to know that the love God has for you and me is a love completely devoid of ulterior motives. God loves us all. He is not merely pretending to love you in order to control you.

To like someone implies that the sentiment will continue as long as what is done is pleasing. There is a certain egotism on the part of the "liker." God never loves in this way. His love for mankind is eternal — an everlasting love.

True love costs.

The love God has for us is unattainable by mere man and its cost is unequaled. The cost to God was that He gave the Son He loved and offered Him up for your salvation. The Son of God became a man so that the sons of men could become children of God.

> For God so loved the world, that He gave His only begotten Son, that whosoever believeth in him should not perish, but have everlasting life (John 3:16).

What an amazing description of the love of God! How can you get to know Him better? Through Him who says, "He who has seen me has seen the Father," Jesus Christ the Lord. Just to look at the Cross is sufficient to tell you how much love God has for you.

The point I want to stress is that true love

costs. God gave all without hope of any personal reward. Who could love like that? Only those who allow the love of God to flow into their hearts.

True change is not external.

On one occasion, I was talking to a man who had been serving a prison sentence for twenty years. He had recognized that he was a sinner and believed that the blood of Jesus was sufficient to cover all his sins, including that of taking the life of another human being.

Having accepted Christ as his own personal Saviour and Lord, this man smiled with gladness of heart and I could feel his sense of profound peace. It was impossible to imagine the kind of person he had been before his conversion. How true it is that the gospel changes lives!

> Therefore if any man be in Christ, he is a new creature: old things are passed away; behold, all things are become new (2 Cor. 5:17).

A young addict once said to me that it was impossible for him ever to change. I agreed.

"You are quite right," I told him. "**You** cannot change. You can't even try and change yourself." There was just **no way** he could change himself.

On the surface you can alter things. The appearance of the ground may change, but in the last analysis it is made of the same material. A man may cease smoking in public, but it does not necessarily mean he has changed, merely that he has altered his behavior.

If God merely wished to alter man's behavior, He could do it. But that would not make us sons and daughters. Instead, we'd be His slaves. God does not want this for you because He loves you. He wants your love, and He will do the rest. When He changes your heart, the heart will lead to changed behavior.

You can see that changing your outward behavior is not sufficient. There is much more to it than just achieving an external behavioral modification. The Lord Jesus Christ is interested in a change of conduct, but only as a consequence of a complete transformation of the heart.

The apostle Paul fulfilled the law to the letter, but it did not satisfy the void in his heart. In spite of finding himself blameless, his life was incomplete. ". . . As for legalistic righteousness, faultless" (Phil. 3:6;NIV) is how he describes himself. Paul's outward behavior was completely acceptable, but it was not enough in the sight of God.

The Jews, at the time Paul was writing, were insisting on complicated ceremonial hand washing and regulations concerning hairstyle and circumcision. All these external things can never quench the thirst for the love of God. That deep desire can only be satisfied by the love of God itself.

. . . I have loved you with an everlasting love; I have drawn you with loving-kindness (Jer. 31:3;NIV).

I hope this helps you understand what I mean by saying that God does not "like" you, He **loves** you. What is more, He loves you as you are, where you are. You do not have to be changed to qualify for His love. If you accept His love, it will undoubtedly change you. When you live in His extraordinary love, you will find a whole new life gushing out, a new life from God himself.

3. God does not "tolerate" you. He accepts you.
Do you think that God only accepts you because He has good reason to? God does not, in fact, have any reason at all for accepting anyone.
He accepts you because He loves you.

> To the praise of the glory of his grace, wherein he hath made us accepted in the beloved (Eph. 1:6).

Secretly, we would really like God to have a good reason for accepting us since this feeds our ego, which is always demanding to be satisfied. In the vanity of our own thinking, nothing would satisfy us more than to think that God has recognized us because we deserve it. The child in each of us would love to think that we are the center of God's attention, but God does not see in anyone the slightest qualification to be recognized!
He gives you recognition out of His goodness

and for the glory of His Holy name. When you understand this fully, it will cause you to mature in your thinking and bring great liberation to you, which is, after all, what you want so badly. To put it another way, it has to be "not I but Christ" who takes your place.

To be tolerated is to be accepted without being loved.

The child who is not loved but merely tolerated simply because he is a "son" will become an insecure person. He will be incapable of loving fully and carry the burden of low self-image throughout life. Only when such a person recognizes his own situation and forgives those who tolerate him without loving him, can he start to live a full and intensely loving life.

Several years ago a young pastor came to ask for help because, as he put it, "No matter how much effort I put in, I will never see revival in my church." I noticed right away that, consciously or unconsciously, he was trying to cover up his real need.

Most people think if you cover up sufficiently well, the problem will disappear or at least become tolerable. But nothing is further from the truth.

I wanted to tell him that the secret of revival is a healthy church. A healthy body reproduces, and if this isn't happening, there is an anomaly somewhere that needs to be diagnosed, excised, and given "post-operative care."

I could have told him that his church needed an experience of healing, next correct teaching, and then preaching. (This in no way contradicts the biblical order of preaching, teaching, and healing, which is the ministry of the Church.) Although revival is important, we also need to heal those we already have in our churches.

Instead of giving him my thoughts on revival, I said, "Let's talk about you for a moment." I wanted to listen to what he had to say about himself first. Listening to people means more than just hearing the sounds; it means listening for what they are **really** saying and seeing that the person himself is important. I wanted this young man to know that I cared about him.

He began to share his strivings, his dreams, and his great love for the Church of the Lord Jesus Christ. In short, I could see a note of deep conviction, of honesty, and of true love for the work of God. However, as he spoke I also began to see anxiety in his bearing.

Anxiety is a cover-up.

Anxiety is a cloak that is often used to cover a deep desire for self-sufficiency and the doubt of achieving it. Self-sufficiency is seen as being a desirable characteristic. However, behind it lies pride. It is the desire to be top of the pile and to show others that they are not needed.

No matter how much the "child" in you makes you think that you don't need anything, you still, in your heart of hearts, know you have the need.

The desire to be someone, but at the same time knowing that it is impossible, creates a deep-seated anxiety.

As we discussed the pastor's background, particularly his childhood, I discovered a terrible vacuum. He had been starved of love without any hope of receiving it from his parents. As a consequence, he lacked the security of knowing that he was loved for himself and not for what he could do. There was just a deep, dark hole.

When he was asking for revival for his church, he was also asking for his own revival. Spiritual revival is a new awareness of God in our lives. It is just like the start of a love affair — full of great expectations. The young minister was really asking for the same experience in his own life, only he did not know it.

I believe his whole intention was for his church, but behind his intention was the need to know who he was. He was one of three brothers, and his father never paid much attention to him. His mother was always "too tired" to notice him. He was there, but that was all. He felt tolerated but not really loved.

I stressed the point that God did not just tolerate him but really loved him. When I said, "Because God loves you, He accepts you as you are," the pastor experienced a deep liberation in his heart. Before this happened, however, he had to free himself from his parents, against whom he had held a grudge for many years. That day something extraordinary happened.

A few weeks later he wrote to me: "I feel wonderfully free, thanks to you and the theotherapy God used so well. Having discovered that my problem was not the lack of revival in my church but that I was in fact the problem, something great has started to happen. Now as I walk down the street and talk about the Lord, people are converted. Even my own family has seen a change in me. The revival I asked for in my church has started with my own revival."

The secret of victory for this young pastor was recognizing that his worth did not depend on what others thought about him but only on what God thought. Once he experienced the love of God, he could begin to love. This was the start of his own revival and that of his church. Joy started to flow like rivers of living water in the life of this young minister.

> . . . If anyone is thirsty, let him come to me and drink. Whoever believes in me, as the Scripture has said, streams of living water will flow from within him (John 7:37-38;NIV).

God does not "tolerate" you. You are loved and totally accepted.

4. Believing in God is not enough. You must BELIEVE GOD.

Confused doctrine creates psychological confusion. This theotherapy principle is based on the fact that we are made up of three parts: spirit, soul, and body.

> May God himself, the God of peace, sanctify you through and through. May your whole spirit, soul and body be kept blameless at the coming of our Lord Jesus Christ. The one who calls you is faithful and he will do it (1 Thess. 5:23;NIV).

Sound theology leads to a sound mind. This principle is at the bottom of every situation you face. In order to have a true relationship with God and good emotional health, you must distinguish between believing in God and **believing God.** In other words, you must believe that God exists somewhere and have faith in Him on a daily basis.

The apostle Paul wrote to Timothy saying, ". . . for I know whom I have believed" (2 Tim. 1:12).

What is the difference between "believing in" and "believing?"

You believe God when you accept that He sent His Son to give His life for you. This is what makes the difference. When most people say "I believe in God," what they really mean is "I believe that God exists," but they do not place their faith in Him in any active way.

In a section of a city occupied by known prostitutes and drug dealers, I asked a group of people how many of them believed in God. All of them did! I asked the same question in a prison, and all of them said they believed in God!

In fact, the phrase "I believe in God" is often used as a cover-up for deep doubts as to who God really is. The expression itself is not necessarily incorrect, but it all depends on what the person using it really means.

If you have learned that your faith is the way you give glory to God, then to confess that you believe in God serves some useful purpose. If, on the other hand, your faith is only something you use in dire circumstances, then your faith is only a way of attempting to manipulate God. The result is that you try to use God instead of giving Him the praise and the glory due Him.

In its plainest form, believing in God merely signifies, "I believe that God exists." If what you really want to say is, "I know that He is God and that is why I praise and glorify Him, and I know that He has perfect control over my life," then your heart will fill with peace.

Perfect peace.

A heart full of peace will automatically bring about emotional health and even promote good physical health. The Bible is full of evidence of this:

> You will keep in perfect peace him whose mind is steadfast, because he trusts in you (Isa. 26:3;NIV).

Your confidence needs to be based not on

what God has done, nor even on what He is going to do, but simply on who He is. David writes, "My hope is in YOU" (Ps. 39:7). When your confidence is in the person of God, then the result is a profound rest that will spare you a great deal of mental energy.

> . . . In repentance and rest is your salvation, in quietness and trust is your strength . . . (Isa. 30:15;NIV).

This trust, or confidence, is to be placed in God and is associated here with inner peace. The one who has true rest is the one who has faith in God for who He is, not for his acts — past, present, or future.

To believe God is to believe that He is able to lead your life in complete rest, no matter how deep the valleys you have to cross. Belief in God, by contrast, implies that God exists and that in order to attract His attention and gain His favor, you have to earn it. This is simply not biblical.

You are now aware of a great truth. Anyone who thinks he has to earn God's attention, or at least work not to lose it, will use up their reservoir of mental energy asking for the joy of His presence. All this psychological energy put to the wrong use will create fatigue, which in turn brings emotional tension and poor physical health.

> Why are you downcast, O my soul? Why so disturbed within me? Put your

hope in God, for I will yet praise him, my Saviour and my God (Ps. 42:11;NIV).

Be still, and know that I am God ... (Ps. 46:10).

I know many people who live with difficult circumstances and conflicts yet they have attained peace and experience the fullest possible enjoyment out of life. Why? Because they understood and applied these principles, and, as a result, a complete transformation took place in their lives.

Deep inner peace is not something you achieve; it is something you receive. All your best endeavors will never achieve peace.

Anyone who has spent hours practicing forms of Eastern meditation in an effort to quell their anxieties and produce peace knows from their own experience that it eludes them. If you are one of those who spends long hours in meditation, then think again. If you have to spend so much time in this way in order to achieve peace, then that implies it is almost impossible for the average man to achieve.

It is far better to consider the words of the One who did not have to spend long hours in meditation to have deep peace because He **is** peace.

Peace I leave with you; my peace I give you. I do not give to you as the world gives. Do not let your hearts be troubled and do not be afraid (John 14:27;NIV).

If only we could all say like the apostle Paul: "I know whom I have believed."

Believe God!

5. God rejects sin but accepts the sinner

A young woman of twenty-eight once told me, "I am divorced. I had a child that I gave up for adoption. I've had an abortion and am now an alcoholic. Is there any hope for me?"

I really wanted to reach out to this wounded young lady and assure her that there was indeed hope, and that God really did love her. This would have been very compassionate but, actually, would not have helped her come to terms with her own attitude of self-pity and constant doubting of God's love for her. This woman needed to discover why she was rejecting herself.

In the last analysis, true rejection is the rejection you express toward yourself. The problem is not God. Indeed, God is **never** the problem. This woman was her own problem because she had a negative attitude toward herself, a distorted concept of God, and a twisted perception of the gospel.

Softly and firmly I encouraged her to talk about herself — not about her divorce or her abortion or her child or her alcoholism — but about **herself**.

She said that she had never known her father. Her mother would come home at all hours of the night, usually drunk, and accompanied by different men each time. All her life this woman had struggled to survive emotionally, searching for someone to love her — not for what she could give but for who she was.

Someone had told her about theotherapy, so she had come to see me. "Now what?" she asked, not so much as a challenge but wondering what her world would bring next.

What I heard her say was very revealing because it is the cry of all humanity. What she meant was, "I am not worthy to be loved, and no one loves me, so how can I ever hope that God would love me?"

I explained the story of the woman caught in adultery in John, Chapter 8:

> The teachers of the law and the Pharisees brought in a woman caught in adultery. They made her stand before the group and said to Jesus, "Teacher, this woman was caught in the act of adultery. In the Law Moses commanded us to stone such women. Now what do you say?" They were using this question as a trap, in order to have a basis for accusing him.
>
> But Jesus bent down and started to write on the ground with his finger. When they kept on questioning him, he straightened up and said to them, "If any one of you is without sin, let him be the first to throw a stone at her." Again he stooped down and wrote on the ground.
>
> At this, those who heard began to go

away one at a time, the older ones first, until only Jesus was left, with the woman standing there. Jesus straightened up and asked her, "Woman, where are they? Has no one condemned you?"

"No one sir," she said.

"Then neither do I condemn you," Jesus declared. "Go now and leave your life of sin" (John 8:3-11;NIV).

Often I see people using their feelings of low self-esteem as an excuse for not dealing with their inner conflicts. They sometimes even use their suffering as a weapon to punish others as well as themselves. It is easier to wallow in self-pity or to speak disparagingly about themselves than to face the cause of their suffering. This does not mean that you should always be looking for someone to blame but rather that you need to unravel the tangled mess.

Tangles do not get straightened out merely by tugging at one end. The mess is not solved by a simple alteration of behavior. There must first of all be a change of heart.

How can the conflicts be solved?

The starting point is to accept that things are not right. You cannot ever expect to straighten out something you do not perceive to be crooked. In the young woman's situation the real conflict was not her alcoholism or abortion or having to give up her child. It wasn't even her divorce. It was

herself; her attitude toward herself, to me, to her world, and finally toward God. At the bottom of it all was her erroneous concept of God.

For her, as for many other people, God was a stern authoritarian father figure, one who must be appeased. Otherwise, He would inflict cruel punishment in return, the kind of authority figure to whom you either submit blindly or pay the price for your rebellion. How far this is from the God of the Bible!

> "Come now, let us reason together," says the Lord. "Though your sins are like scarlet, they shall be white as snow; though they are red as crimson, they shall be like wool" (Isa. 1:18;NIV).

This woman finally understood that the gospel was not just fine-sounding, empty words. The gospel of the Lord Jesus Christ is an invitation to live the life of the kingdom of God here on Earth with the certain hope of eternal life. This is the life the Lord Jesus Christ came to teach us to live.

Your worth does not depend on what you have nor even on what you are. It depends on what God makes of you. God took Saul of Tarsus, the Pharisee, self-righteous blasphemer, persecutor of the Church, and transformed him into the apostle Paul who wrote: "For to me to live is Christ, and to die is gain" (Phil. 1:21).

The young woman understood for the first time in her life that the image she had of herself was just a shadow of what she could be or become. She began to see herself from another perspective — God's viewpoint — and was born again.

Her heart changed, and today she is happy. Jesus is much more to her than someone found in the pages of the Bible who lived many years ago. Now Jesus is her all-sufficient Saviour and the Lord of her life.

> But God demonstrates his own love
> for us in this: While we were still sinners,
> Christ died for us (Rom. 5:8;NIV).

Yes, Jesus rejects sin, but He accepts the sinner with love. He hates divorce but loves the divorcee. He hates homosexuality but loves the homosexual.

He loves you, and he loves me, and to everyone He says: ". . . Then neither do I condemn you. Go . . . Go now and leave your life of sin" (John 8:11;NIV).

6. God does not just look at you. He sees everything.

There is a saying that the worst sin a man can commit against another is to look at him without seeing him. Jesus asked, "Do you have eyes but fail to see, and ears but fail to hear . . .?" (Mark 8:18;NIV).

People will often project onto others their own values, faults, and even suspicions. Sometimes they will act indifferently toward others. This can be a weapon against fear, particularly to fend off those things that threaten them. The use of indifference in a threatening situation avoids confrontation.

These two mechanisms can even be used against God himself. Many times in our fear, either real or imagined, we project onto God our own feelings. One of the most common fears is that you are not important enough for God to see you. You feel that He may look at you, but He would not actually take any notice.

This feeling is not usually expressed in a direct way but more commonly as a subtle thought such as, "God is too busy to see me" or "God helps those who help themselves." Behind these expressions, you will find the sense of something missing, a nagging doubt about the person's own sense of worthiness.

Why is there such a tendency to underestimate oneself?
As a general rule the cause can be traced to the events of the formative years and the experience of childhood, when one or more significant adults failed to love and accept you as they should have.

When a child is not taken seriously, he will assume, as he grows up, that his worth is limited and that it depends on good behavior. The automatic result of this is a poor self-image, which is diametrically opposed to what God, who actually does know every detail of your life, actually says of you.

And even the very hairs of your head

are all numbered. So don't be afraid; you are worth more than many sparrows (Matt. 10:30;NIV).

The meaning of the original Greek goes one step further. Not only does God know the total quantity of the hairs of your head, but if one is missing He knows precisely which one. We are not just numbers in a celestial file but very important and very significant to God.

In general, the opinion you have of yourself is conditioned by the opinion others have of you. However, the emotionally mature person is the one who forms his own opinion of himself without basing it on what others think of him. In order to have a good self-image you must confront and deal with your basic insecurities.

The child without a secure upbringing will obviously grow up insecure and, therefore, tend to base his opinion of himself on what others think. Insecurity, the fear of not being acceptable, has its roots in feelings of latent guilt or in the careless remarks of others.

The Bible has a very clear message about this area and one of the most wonderful passages is when God says: ". . . Let us make man in our image, after our likeness . . ." (Gen. 1:26).

You, the reader of this book, are important.
It does not matter whether you have achieved a lot or nothing at all. What matters is that you have been created in the image of God himself. David was

meditating about this thought when he wrote:

> What is man that you are mindful of him, or the son of man that you care for him? You made him a little lower than the heavenly beings and crowned him with glory and honor (Ps. 8:4-5;NIV).

In Puerto Rico, many children roam the streets, looking for ways to make money. One day as I went shopping and parked the car, a young boy offered to look after my automobile for five pence, so I agreed. When I returned, he told me that he had done his duty. I decided to give him the benefit of the doubt and gave him five single pennies as the agreed rate.

To my surprise, he angrily threw the five pennies on the ground and demanded a five pence piece. I realized immediately that he needed something more than the money from me. I picked up the coins and offered to buy him a cola so I could get change and give him his five pence piece.

Afterwards the lad said, "Mister, I'll look after your car anytime, whenever you go shopping, and you don't owe me anything!"

This little episode shows rather well how we, as human beings, need to feel important. Only when we feel like "someone" can we begin to love ourselves.

When visiting South America some years ago, an American sociologist mentioned during my stay the "gamins," children abandoned by their parents, quite literally. He noted that the gamins were totally devoid of any emotion and quite unable to love.

That describes the end result of a total lack of love. You cannot love genuinely unless you yourself have been loved. Thank God, He loved us before we even knew Him: "We love him, because he first loved us" (1 John 4:19).

The greatest discovery you can make is to know that you are the object of God's love, not because of your achievements or because of who you are, but simply because He loves you. Once you discover this truth for yourself, your concept of yourself will change overnight.

One day an ex-judge came to my office as part of his search to find himself. He had turned to alcohol and said, "You **must** help me."

His attitude was very positive in that he acknowledged his need of help. After talking some time I asked him to repeat this simple prayer after me:

Lord, thank You for loving me so much. Now I understand that if I had been the only person on the face of the whole Earth, You would still have gone to the Cross just for me. I knew that You loved me but never realized before quite how much You love me. Thank You, Lord.

The judge paused for a while, deep in thought, as if he had been hypnotized by the prayer. He then asked in a tone of amazement, "Do you mean to say, that is really how much God loves me?"

"Yes, Sir, that's how much God loves you." There was no more to be said.

When God looks at you, He sees you through and through. As you see your value to Him, it enables you to walk tall and face life.

> Who is it that overcomes the world?
> Only he who believes that Jesus is the Son
> of God (1 John 5:5;NIV).

4

Doing First Things First

You will never become more than you now are unless you go beyond where you are to the maximum of your own potential. I can hear you wondering, "How can I possibly do that?"

It is done simply by learning to establish priorities. You need to decide out of all the alternatives in your life what is the most important thing to do. Then you need to do it first and to the best of your ability.

"Seek ye first the kingdom of God" is far more than just a well-known verse and instruction. It is an extraordinarily valuable biblical principle that is both spiritually and psychologically of great importance.

The inability or avoidance of establishing priorities can be a major source of tension in our lives.

I remember one time when I tried to make a long distance phone call. The operator at the other end turned out to be a recorded message that said, "All lines are engaged. Please try again later."

It can be just like that with our minds. All the lines are jammed with innumerable tasks, engagements, dates, meetings, needs, bills to pay, emergencies, until there is no room for new input.

> Therefore do not worry about tomorrow, for tomorrow will worry about itself. Each day has enough trouble of its own (Matt. 6:34;NIV).

When you have too much to take in all at once, it is obvious you need to establish priorities. The danger to beware of, however, is putting off things that could and should be done immediately while you are assessing the priorities.

"Do It Tomorrow"

Deferring a decision can be the result of an unconscious fear of being unable to achieve something. It brings with it anxiety and a feeling of guilt. If you are one of those with a recurring tendency to "put it off until tomorrow," then underneath lies a deep insecurity and fear of failure.

This fear of failure is fed by the constant need for approval from someone you regard as important. You feel compelled to please him or her to avoid being rejected.

This reminds me of a young man who came to see me and said, "I have great enthusiasm whenever I start anything new and get cracking with a great dedication to the task. After a while, however, I quit and start something else, and then the same thing happens all over again."

When the root of the problem was exposed, he could see that the battle was over his tendency to "do it tomorrow." He felt in his heart of hearts that his father, whom he admired greatly, would reject him if he didn't excel in all he set out to do. The boy's admiration for his father had created a giant of a man whose stature the son could never match.

Unconsciously, he had made a decision never to complete anything he had started because, if he finished the job, he might then discover he had not reached his father's standard. By leaving the end result in doubt, he avoided the final comparison. It was less painful to quit than to leave open the possibility of failure. This young man was playing a game that many people participate in to avoid confronting a sense of inadequacy.

For it is: Do and do, do and do, rule on rule, rule on rule; a little here, a little there (Isa. 28:10;NIV).

The tendency to postpone things denotes an exaggerated dependency on the approval of others while at the same time fearing that their approval will not be forthcoming.

The root cause of such insecurity can usually

be found in the attitude of approval shown by one of the significant adults in the person's formative childhood years.

Exposing Hidden Fears

Countless Christians end up seeing their minister, or even a psychiatrist, because they have lost their faith. They don't realize that behind the loss of interest in spiritual things lies hidden fears. Once these fears are exposed to the light of the gospel, they lose their power to block a person's faith.

You, dear children, are from God and have overcome them, because the one who is in you is greater than the one who is in the world (1 John 4:4;NIV).

God has not called you to be great angels in the heavens, nor has He called you to be a mediocre human being on the Earth. He has called you to be nothing less than a mature man or woman in His Son, the Lord Jesus Christ.

You will seek me and find me when you seek me with all your heart (Jer. 29:13;NIV).

But seek first his kingdom and his righteousness, and all these things will be given to you as well (Matt. 6:33;NIV).

Learn from the example of Jesus on the cross. As He was fulfilling the plan for your salvation, He resisted the temptation to put it off and avoid facing the necessity of going through with it. You, too, need to learn to do the most important things first, and do them well, as unto the Lord.

5

How to Be Happy All the Time

It is often said that perfect happiness does not exist. We are so accustomed to this way of thinking that we live without really being aware whether we are happy or not.

What is true happiness? How can you be truly happy **all** of the time?

We need to start by seeing what happiness is not. It is not the absence of problems, conflicts, or unpleasant situations. There are, of course, those who do equate happiness with the absence of problems, and I expect you know such people.

The Bible, however, has something quite different to say on the matter. Jesus himself said: ". . . In this world you will have trouble. But take heart! I have overcome the world" (John 16:33;NIV).

This passage clearly indicates that happiness is not the absence of difficulties. We all know people whom we would describe as happy, yet all the while they are dealing with difficult situations such as illness, conflicts with the children, afflictions of various kinds, or financial setbacks. Despite their circumstances, however, they remain truly happy people.

Is Money Everything?

Happiness does not consist of material possessions either. Many people are under the misapprehension that economic prosperity is an indispensable ingredient of true happiness.

We all know the saying, "Money isn't everything ... but it helps!" I would even go so far as to say that the very opposite is true. It is only when you have rid yourself of the desire for possessions that you are even capable of experiencing true happiness.

The desire for material goods is a snare that constantly traps many, many people. If you think about it a little longer, you will realize that it is, in fact, impossible for something tangible in the form of a possession to produce something intangible like happiness.

And I'll say to myself, "You have plenty of good things laid up for many years. Take life easy; eat, drink and be merry." But God said to him, "You fool! This very night your life will be demanded from you. Then who will get what you have prepared for yourself?"

This is how it will be with anyone who stores up things for himself but is not rich toward God (Luke 12:19-21;NIV).

Learning to live an abundant life without depending on what you can or cannot have will bring, as an inevitable result, true happiness. Paul describes it like this:

. . . I have learned to be content whatever the circumstances. I know what it is to be in need, and I know what it is to have plenty. I have learned the secret of being content in any and every situation, whether well fed or hungry, whether living in plenty or in want (Phil. 4:11-12;NIV).

Paul learned the secret. So can we.

The Search for Happiness

Others look for happiness through acquiring a high degree of culture or knowledge. Many people think that they will only be really happy once they have obtained some high academic achievement. There is plenty of evidence to show this futile way of thinking.

Puerto Rico, where I live, for example, claims one of the highest literacy rates in the world. Yet even with this high level of education, it has one of the greatest rates of per capita alcohol consumption anywhere in the world!

If happiness were to be found solely in education, then you would expect Puerto Rico to be one of the happiest places in the world. Instead, 25 percent of the population are so miserable they are addicted either to alcohol or drugs.

This should show us quite clearly that those who seek happiness for its own sake actually end up with quite the reverse! Certainly nothing the world has to offer will ever bring happiness because happiness is not something you possess. It is something you are. In other words, you don't **have** happiness, you **are** happy.

Humanist thinking would like us to believe that we can achieve happiness through our own efforts. This, too, is wrong.

> For I resolved to know nothing while I was with you except Jesus Christ and him crucified (1 Cor. 2:2;NIV).

The Book of Ecclesiastes is an excellent source of truth, and it unequivocally confirms all that I have shared with you — namely that man cannot achieve happiness by his own efforts.

> I, the Teacher, was king over Israel in Jerusalem. I devoted myself to study and to explore by wisdom all that is done under heaven. What a heavy burden God has

laid on men! I have seen all the things that are done under the sun; all of them are meaningless, a chasing after the wind (Eccles. 1:12-14;NIV).

A little further on the teacher, in his constant search for happiness, comes to understand this truth:

I thought in my heart, "Come now, I will test you with pleasure to find out what is good." But that also proved to be meaningless. "Laughter," I said, "is foolish. And what does pleasure accomplish?" (Eccles. 2:1-2;NIV).

Obviously, happiness is not merely the absence of problems, nor is it the result of having material comforts or obtaining a great deal of knowledge. Happiness is not something you can possess.

What is True Happiness?

How then can happiness be attained? We have already seen that it is not what you have, but what you are. We need to learn to distinguish between **being happy** and just **being in pleasant circumstances.** One is a state of being, an internal spiritual condition, that influences and determines our emotional state but is not dependent on external circumstances; the other is wholly dependent on external factors.

It is true that a certain satisfaction is attained by being in comfortable surroundings, but it actually depends on being in them, and, therefore, cannot be called true happiness. In other words, we can be comfortable without being happy. We can also be happy even if deprived of comfortable surroundings.

Happiness is the work of God in our hearts. Consider this biblical definition of happiness:

> May God himself, the God of peace, sanctify you through and through. May your whole spirit, soul and body be kept blameless at the coming of our Lord Jesus Christ (1 Thess. 5:23;NIV).

Happiness is first and foremost a spiritual state. The **spirit** always looks at the things that are eternal. The **soul,** which is the seat of the emotions, reason, and the will, has had experiences in the past and is affected by unconscious processes. The **body** is only concerned with the present — with what is happening here and now.

True happiness is attainable because it depends neither on the past nor on the present, but on that which is to come.

> Since, then, you have been raised with Christ, set your hearts on things above, where Christ is seated at the right hand of God. Set your minds on things above, not

on earthly things (Col. 3:1-2;NIV).

Happiness is a spiritual state that influences our emotional and even our physical state. This happiness affects our state of mind and is not dependent on outward circumstances. Rather, it depends solely on the security that comes from having your eyes fixed on the Lord.

> Let us fix our eyes on Jesus, the author and perfector of our faith, who for the joy set before him endured the cross, scorning its shame, and sat down at the right hand of the throne of God (Heb. 12:2;NIV).

From the moment I learned from the Word of God that perfect happiness was indeed possible, I have experienced it continually.

If you read the Beatitudes in Matthew 5, substituting the word"happy" for "blessed," it becomes obvious that true happiness has a deeper source than man can achieve or possess.

Consider those people Jesus called happy: the poor, the grieving, the meek, those wanting righteousness, the merciful, the pure in heart, the peacemakers, those persecuted for righteousness and for His sake. These people would certainly not "feel happy" if happiness depended on their circumstances.

Permanent Joy

Happiness or joy is the result of knowing deep within our beings that we have been forgiven by God, that we have been accepted by Him, and that He loves us unconditionally. God himself has promised that we will be blessed and happy.

> Be strong and courageous. Do not be afraid or terrified because of them, for the Lord you God goes with you; he will never leave you nor forsake you (Deut. 31:6;NIV).

This state of happiness and joy is permanent, whereas contentment or cheerfulness can only be temporary. Happiness flows from the inside outward, while cheerfulness flows from an outside experience inward. Joy results from looking to God; cheerfulness comes from yourself. Circumstances do not dictate happiness; they can only bring cheerfulness or contentment.

Happiness produces a level of joy which, when internalized, becomes part of the personality and is converted into strength. "... The joy of the Lord is your strength (Neh. 8:10;NIV).

This joy is the very life of Jesus in our hearts and "the fruit of the Spirit is . . . joy . . ." (Gal. 5:22;NIV).

This kind of happiness is not a temporary state but a permanent condition that is independent of outside circumstances. Hence, it is quite possible to cry and still be happy, or not to cry and be sad. Jesus himself wept (John 11:35). Although tears are an outward expression of a deep feeling inside, they do not affect happiness. Even though a person is experiencing a temporary state of deep emotion, in the depth of his being that person can remain completely happy.

I can remember my feelings at my mother's funeral. In the midst of the grief produced by the death of one I loved so dearly, I could both weep and have peace that she was in the hands of God. How is it possible to be happy in the midst of conflicts? This only happens when we learn to deal with the conflicts that caused things to go wrong in the first place. For this we need to learn more about the nature of the conflicts themselves.

We are our own problem. This principle can be applied to every area of our lives. How we feel about situations and what the circumstances actually are can be two completely different things. Once we grasp this, we can acknowledge that it is possible to look at the circumstances without allowing them to influence our happiness. We can be objective in assessing our feelings.

We become the problem when we allow our circumstances to determine our state of mind. When we are truly happy, then we can say from our hearts: "I have been crucified with Christ and I no longer live, but Christ lives in me" (Gal. 2:20;NIV).

If you want to be able to say this, then you need to open your heart to the Lord and say, "Lord, I need You in my life and I ask You to take control of it. I hand it over to You."

You need to get into reading the Bible and attending a church fellowship where they acknowledge the lordship of Jesus and desire to be Christlike.

Yes, it is possible for you to be completely happy all of the time, and as a truly happy person you can bring happiness to others.

6

Living a Quality Life

God's plan for us is to experience a life so full of vitality and interest that it touches others and changes them. This is the quality of life He wants to give us.

> I have come that they might have life, and that they might have it more abundantly (John 10:10).

The popular saying "live and let live" suggests a philosophy of life that covers over a deep egotism and shows a false idea of service. It is the same as saying, "What happens to you doesn't matter to me, as long as it's not happening to me." In others words, your experience will not be the same as mine.

"What will be will be." The feeling behind this kind of attitude is one of selfishness, which is always dehumanizing.

The Lord teaches us:

Heal the sick, raise the dead, cleanse those who have leprosy, drive out demons. Freely you have received, freely give (Matt. 10:8;NIV).

The love Jesus gave was real love:

For God so loved the world, that he gave his only begotten Son, that whosoever believeth in him should not perish, but have everlasting life (John 3:16).

Love always gives. You can, of course, give without love, but you cannot love without giving. The rich man who gives money to the beggar does not have to love him. Equally, the beggar can give without love.

When you love you give. It is inevitable and an integral part of love. This is why true love promotes emotional well-being. There is no more practical way of showing love to others than to talk to them about the Lord Jesus Christ. His love is firm, constant, unchanging, sincere, honest, and true.

Love is patient, love is kind. It does not envy, it does not boast, it is not proud.

It is not rude, it is not self-seeking, it is not easily angered, it keeps no record of wrongs. Love does not delight in evil but rejoices with the truth. It always protects, always trusts, always hopes, always perseveres (1 Cor. 13:4-7;NIV).

True love does not control, dictate, make demands, or impose a standard of expected behavior.

Selfish Love

Often when we say to someone "I love you," we think we are meaning the agape type of love. However, true **agape** love and selfish **phileo** love are two quite different sentiments.

Phileo love is what we do when we want something for ourselves. If it is expressed with hands together and pointing toward ourselves, this gesture implies we are the center and object of that love.

Selfish love is the characteristic of a child. It is quite reasonable for a baby to know what it wants when it wants it. A lot of tears will be shed before he changes. That's the way it is since he is the object of his own desire, and this behavior is necessary for his survival. The child's tears produce in us the urgent desire to satisfy his need immediately. The baby does not cry for the future but only for the need of the moment.

Selfish love imposes conditions, such as "I

will only give you what you want provided you give me something" or "I will please you if you will please me."

Phileo love is always egocentric, selfish, and demanding. Those who love in this way impose their own conditions and are only really interested in controlling the situation as a result. It is worth adding that sex in marriage can be motivated by the child or the adult in us, either by phileo love or agape love.

True mature love does not make demands. It has only one condition, namely: not to make any conditions. As soon as love starts to become conditional and demanding, it ceases being true agape love and turns into phileo love.

We love when the object of our affection is outside ourselves and when the only reward is to love. If love does not bring with it sufficient joy from that love, then we need to examine ourselves to see the real motive behind our actions.

The father who says to his son, "If you're a good boy and behave well, then I'll take you to the circus," is teaching him phileo love and not agape love. The end result is that he will become selfish and self-centered. This kind of behavior may well result in his son becoming "macho," arrogant, assertive, proud, and definitely not a good husband.

A parent should just tell his child to behave properly without having to offer a reward. Good behavior is its own reward. When we learn that particular rewards determine our behavior, it robs us of our joy and our happiness in discovering ourselves. We must not fail to see that doing good is in itself its own reward.

Genuine Love

When we love genuinely, we are not restricted by seeing others living a better life than ourselves. Instead, we are free to help them live an even fuller life. This is the fundamental biblical reason for evangelism.

Why should we be eager for people to be converted to the Lord? Why should we be preoccupied with their salvation? Because we know that only the Lord Jesus Christ can bring salvation to a man's heart and that only He can bring true happiness.

Authentic love forces us to move out, motivates us, and leads us to others to love. It is not enough to live and let live. It is a precious thing to live and help others to live, too. Love is concerned that others are also happy. This is way we evangelize and speak to others about Christ.

The only true motivation for preaching the gospel is "For the love of Christ constraineth us . . ." (2 Cor. 5:14). ". . . We implore you on Christ's behalf: Be reconciled to God" (2 Cor. 5:20;NIV). Our love encourages others to reach out for the gospel, too.

When a man simply lives and lets live instead of helping others to live, he becomes insensitive to the needs of others around him. This, in turn, changes him into a feeble character who is selfish, insecure, and sterile. He cannot express humility but exalts himself with arrogance. He is the person who lacks self-control because he cannot exercise dominion over his true self.

He is the man, woman, youngster, or child who does not have a clear sense of justice because he does not respect himself or others either. He does not keep his promise because he does not value or love himself. He does not play fair and, as a result, is judged for it, even if he does not really want to cheat.

He lacks courage in the face of danger, and he is not courageous in facing the pressures of life. He is afraid of being on his own because he has not learned to enjoy his own company nor to delight himself in the presence of God.

When we fulfill the Lord's command to preach the gospel, we are helping others to develop their Christian character. This is the responsibility of every believer in the Lord Jesus Christ. It is not enough for you just to live. You need to live helping others. This is your duty and if you will do it, you will discover the healing principle of the words of Jesus himself:

> . . . It is more blessed to give than to receive (Acts 20:35).

Live, helping others to live.

7

Psychological Defenses

Because of his weakness, man erects defenses, or psychological barriers, in the hope that others will not see him as he really is. The irony is that those very defenses are actually the way we show others what we want to conceal!

Accepting our faults, in fact, improves our status with others. However, the weak character frequently has to justify himself. He is constantly defending himself in his struggle but never confronts himself with the problem.

One of the fundamental principles of theotherapy is that psychological defenses actually prevent the spiritual growth and emotional well-being of a person because they dehumanize him.

A good example of this degrading, dehumanizing process, and how it affects one's relationship with God, is found in the Book of Malachi.

The Seven Insolent Questions

Let us look at what I call the seven insolent questions asked by the rebellious people of Israel.

1. They question God's love. "'I have loved you,' says the Lord. But you ask, 'How have you loved us?'" (Mal. 1:2;NIV).
To question God in this way reflects a weak character and a very poor perception of God himself.

2. A little further on God speaks like a tender-hearted father to his rebellious son, but his children respond with insolence.

> "A son honors his father, and a servant his master. If I am a father, where is the honor due me? If I am a master, where is the respect due to me?" says the Lord Almighty.
> "It is you, O priests, who show contempt for my name.
> "But you ask, 'How have we shown contempt for your name?'" (Mal. 1:6;NIV).

3. God continues the dialogue with His people. He tells them how they have dishonored His name:

"You place defiled food on my altar.
"But you ask, 'How have we defiled you?'" (Mal. 1:7;NIV).

The people show that they have no fear of God. Although God does not want us to be afraid of Him, He does want us to try and make Him Lord of our worship and every activity in our lives. This is impossible for the self-centered person because the center of his life is already himself and not God.

4. God speaks to His people again,

You have wearied the Lord with your words.
"How have we wearied him?" you ask (Mal. 2:17;NIV).

5. When God says to them,

". . . Return to me, and I will return to you," says the Lord Almighty. "But you ask, 'How are we to return?'" (Mal. 3:7;NIV).

Once again pride comes to the surface. The arrogant person typically cannot accept responsibility because he is uncertain of his own worth.

The cure for pride is brokenness. So often we do not understand the reason for our suffering and, as a result, question God. The best thing you can do with your suffering is to lay it on the altar and say to the Lord, "Lord, what do You want me to do with this suffering?" When we can do this, our pride is broken and the love of God can flow freely through our lives.

6. God turns to speak to His people and this time confronts them with their sin and selfishness:

"Will a man rob God? Yet you rob me. But you ask, 'How do we rob you?' In tithes and offerings" (Mal. 3:8;NIV).

The people responded with a defensive reply, not acknowledging their wrongdoing.

Giving is the best way of demonstrating love. When we are unable to give, we should examine our so-called love.

7. God continues confronting His people. In the last analysis, the true confrontation is not with the external things but with ourselves.

"You have said harsh things against me," says the Lord.

"Yet you ask, 'What have we said against you?'" (Mal. 3:13;NIV).

These seven insolent questions are indicative of weak people who fear confrontation. This is why they defend themselves with questions.

The **flesh** is arrogant and questions because it

does not want to accept discipline nor to be taught.

The **spirit,** on the other hand, is meek and submissive and if it questions, it is only in order to believe.

We can learn and we can also do better. We can begin by starting to understand ourselves and to understand others.

8

Healing Deep Wounds

The subconscious mind retains the memory of experiences that have been particularly painful and does not allow them to rise to the surface and become consciously remembered. They remain in what is called the "active past."

We cannot go back into the past, of course, and can only remember these memories once they have surfaced into the conscious mind. Man would often like to go back as actors do in science fiction movies — with a time machine that transports people into a bygone era. In reality we know that we cannot go back into the past.

The Lord Jesus Christ, however, is able to change the remembrance of the past and make sense of everything that has happened, including those occurrences in the womb even before birth.

The Lord Jesus Christ can give health to the body, peace to the soul, and life to the spirit.

Jesus Christ is the same yesterday, today, and forever (Heb. 13:8).

The Lord is not limited by time. He can change both time and space at any stage of your life. He can place His hand on the wound or rejection at the precise moment in your life when you received it and heal it immediately.

We need to understand how the Lord can heal wounds caused in infancy or adolescence, or even in adulthood. The following diagram will help:

Negative Active Past . . . Present . . . Future

We need to bear in mind that the aim is not to forget the past but to deactivate it from affecting you adversely. In other words, you need to remove from the past the pain of the memory. Only then will you become free from the negative influence of the past in your present.

O death, where is your sting . . .? (1 Cor. 15:55).

In the same way that death has lost its sting, the past loses its negative power over you once the hand of Jesus takes away the hurts of the past and brings you into freedom.

"So if the Son sets you free, you will be free indeed" (John 8:36;NIV).

Only when we are in Christ is it possible for us to go where He can go. Only He can change what has happened in our past.

Because we are in Him, we can find the little child that represents our life in our formative years. We can be present to receive from the hand of Jesus the healing of our past hurts and rejections.

How wonderful this truth is! It shows that the Bible is neither a book of good advice and wonderful dissertations on the hereafter nor a nice study for Christians on how life will be "on the other side." Instead, the Bible is God's blueprint for an abundant life here and now.

This abundant life includes adjustments and traumas, facing up to conflicts, and the acquiring of a faith to produce mature men and women.

The kingdom of God is not a beautiful country somewhere up in heaven but a practical down-to-earth reality. It is here on Earth where men and women have to live for Christ.

It is time that Christians began to be what they truly are and stop pretending to be what they are not. By surrounding themselves with the mantle of easy religiosity, they throw away what should be their covering — the joy of the Lord. We should recognize our faults without the enemy having us believe that is all there is.

It is not enough to recognize our mistakes. We

need to recognize the efficacy of the blood of the Lord Jesus Christ to cleanse us from all sin.

"... Greater is he that is in you, than he that is in the world" (1 John 4:4).

9

Daring to Live in Intimacy

Stop living in denial.

Denial is, in the last analysis, fear of intimacy: intimacy with God, with others, but most of all, fear of intimacy with oneself.

Daring to live in intimacy means having the courage to stop and examine our motives. Why do you act the way you do? If instead of reacting to our circumstances, we stop and consider what there is in those circumstances that makes us fear self-examination, we may discover why we act the way we act. Let us examine some examples.

Carl complains that his wife is cold, unexpressive, and emotionally uninviting.

Ruth, his wife, on the other hand, complains, "Carl treats me like dirt. He makes me think that I am not good enough."

In this interaction, we notice immediately that there is no meaningful communication. No needs are being met, and fear of intimacy is apparent.

What is the denial? Fear to see oneself as one really is and the consequence, which is fear of rejection. Carl feels rejected, and Ruth feels rejected. Both are craving attention. Neither is addressing the real issue, thus their denial.

The question arises: Does Carl reject Ruth, thus causing her to be cold, unresponsive, etc., or is Ruth's unresponsiveness the cause of Carl's rejection?

Daring to live in intimacy is having the courage to face ourselves in the light of what Jesus Christ has already done on the cross at Calvary. It also means being honest enough to face what needs to be faced and making corrections when necessary. Trying to do this in our own ability is an impossible task.

As we learn more and more that "God so loved us that He gave His only begotten Son" on our behalf, we develop the courage and the self-acceptance to dare to be honest with ourselves, with God, and with others.

There are two principles that, when taken together, can help us overcome the barriers of loneliness and the despair of emotional barrenness, which is the incapacity to live in contact with our true feelings.

1. Re-experience the pain.
The first principle was expressed by a young

Guatemalan preacher when he said that he didn't know his father until he was sixteen years of age. Such was his deep need to "know his father" that he fantasized by imagining that any man who came his way was his father. For sixteen years he lived in a desperate search for a father who was not there.

Then, on his sixteenth birthday, he was told that his father was going to visit him. The boy's life was filled with an unimaginable expectation of what this meeting would be like. He figured that his father would put his arms around him and kiss him and reward him with the loving warmth he had waited sixteen years to receive.

On the day of the meeting, the boy saw a man approach him rather coldly. When he was at a speaking distance from him, the man merely said, "I am your father." He then tapped his son on the shoulder and walked away. That was it. This young man stood there, gripped by the pain of rejection. For years afterward, he was unable to relate to any man and certainly not to God as Father.

It wasn't until this young man was able to touch his feelings of rejection, to "own his loneliness," that he was able to be set free of his fear of intimacy.

We cannot heal what we do not feel. By the same token we cannot forgive unless we feel the pain caused by the act we wish to forgive. We need to know exactly what it is that we are forgiving, but we also need to feel its pain and re-experience its emotional impact.

As this young man re-experienced the pain of that disappointing meeting with his father, his need for intimacy surfaced. Then he was able to understand, for the first time in his life, that God was his real Father and that he was never going to feel abandoned again.

2. Intimacy is threatening.

The second principle was shown to me through a counselor. She was a woman in her late forties, stout, and with a superficial smile on her face. She was hurting but preferred to pretend that she was not. During counseling, she came to the realization that as a small child her emotional needs had not been adequately met by her parents. Her mother, who was a suspicious (paranoid) person, was incapable of expressing her own feelings freely.

Because of her painful childhood, this counselor had buried the heartache and lived in a world of pretense. She "assumed" that others loved her, but deep inside she felt rejected. During the process of counseling, she discovered what I call the second principle to help us overcome the barrier to intimacy: Intimacy is threatening.

When we have lived most of our life with a sense of not being accepted or wanted, this causes a need to protect ourselves from being hurt. The pain of rejection is very deep and very real. It stimulates in us a feeling of low self-esteem, of uselessness, and of meaninglessness. Eventually it causes depression. Just considering opening our heart before another person becomes a frightening thought.

The only way we are able to survive is to seek refuge in our own little sanctuary and just watch the rest of the world go by. If, however, our loneliness is more painful than the pain of breaking out of our shell, we will seek help. At that point, we take a "leap of faith" and decide we want to overcome the fear of intimacy.

When we dare to look into ourselves, we discover it is not as horrible as we thought. We discover that we have value, that life is a gift, and that we can still move forward.

Overcoming the fear of intimacy requires courage and determination.

Eight Steps to Healing the Fear of Intimacy

The need for intimacy is common to us all. In helping people overcome their fear of intimacy, I have found the following eight steps very helpful. The reader may know of other ways.

1. Recognize the need.

Sometimes the real need remains hidden. We know that something is basically wrong, but we do not quite know how to put our finger on the cause.

To do this often requires the help of a trained professional. Pastors, Christian counselors, physicians, or other health professionals can assist us. The bottom line is that the need must be identified before we proceed further.

2. Touch the hurt; be aware of the feelings.

Without touching your feelings, there can be no healing. We must "own our own feelings." Often we are afraid to touch our emotions for fear of the pain that evoking such emotions can cause.

Let me give the reader good news concerning touching the emotions. The moment you get in touch with the emotions they begin to be diffused, and pain begins to disappear immediately.

3. Share your feelings.

As you express deep-seated feelings, fear dissipates. It is like turning on the light in the dark. The moment this is done fears dissipate because now you can "see."

4. Diffuse the feelings.

Diffusion comes when you bring conflicts into the light and you begin to look at each conflict individually and objectively. You see things for what they are and not for what you thought they were or for what others may have made you think they were.

Diffusion means that you separate feelings from facts and fantasy from reality. As you begin to see things as they really are, you begin to get a grip on facts and let go of fears and false concepts.

5. Dealing with your fear of intimacy is to recognize the resulting behavior.

You acted as a result of fear, and the result was isolation and depression. Now you begin to act as a result of new insights. You see things as they are and no longer as you "felt" them to be. What a sense of freedom this brings!

"Then you will know the truth, and the truth will set you free" (John 8:32;NIV) is a deeply healing principle.

6. Alter present behavior.

One recommendation that has proved extremely useful to many of my counselors through the years is to cultivate a consistent and meaningful devotional life.

Learn to talk with God as you would talk with a friend. Make this a priority in your life. Read a verse or two of Scripture and ponder over what it means to you. You will be amazed at what this daily practice will do for you.

7. Share your healing with others.

As you begin to experience your intimacy with God and with yourself, and as you become more in touch with your own feelings, let other people know. In the process you will develop intimacy with others as well. What a peace this gives.

You see, as you begin to get close to others, you begin to meet their needs. You become a channel of God's love for others.

8. Grow in grace (2 Thess. 2:1).

Do not stay stagnant. Every day is an opportunity for growth. Lean heavily on the Lord Jesus Christ for your strength.

Join a support group. A church that preaches the Word and is guided by the Holy Spirit is the best support group in the world. Join! Become an active participant rather than a passive spectator. Enjoy the process.

Thousands attest to the efficacy of these steps in bringing about a release from the fear of intimacy. I pray that you will be one more.

10

You Can Start Again

From the moment of conception, a person is affected by the external events that affect the mother and produce in her emotions that are not always positive or healthy. These emotions are then transmitted to the baby being formed within her.

Birth itself is a traumatic experience for the baby. In the womb, the fetus lacks nothing. There is nourishment without having to cry, constant temperature control, pleasant darkness, a floating place of rest, and perfect hygiene. On entering the world, the child encounters a hostile environment where he has to struggle to live.

In his early years, all sorts of disagreeable situations may occur to mar the sensitivity of the developing child. Then in adolescence, puberty arrives, and the child begins to develop negative habits and antisocial attitudes.

These habits and attitudes are then carried

over into adulthood where frustrations encountered by adjusting to life, job insecurities, and broken relationships result in a life that seems beyond their control to fix.

The good news for you, however, is that you can start all over again. Over the last twenty-five years, I have had the privilege of seeing thousands of young men and women make a new start in life and become successful in the very areas where they had feared failure.

Many were devoid of stability and their self-esteem had reached rock bottom. Others had lost all hope of regaining good family relationships, of taking a particular course of study, or of becoming financially stable again or even for the first time. When they laid hold of the biblical principles and correct thinking, their lives were transformed and they now experience joy and victory.

How can you start afresh? Following are listed some truths that will help you stay on tract.

1. You will rarely feel loved by the whole world.

That is the plain fact of the matter. There will be times when even the people who love you, will give the impression they couldn't care less. That does not mean you are not loved nor that it is beneath you to need to be loved.

Sometimes those you truly love will get the impression that you do not love them, even though you do. When this happens, when you get that feeling or give the impression of not loving, pause for a moment and then start again.

2. You will not always triumph.

There will be times in your life when you are going to fail. Remember that failure is simply triumph in reverse. The Psalmist reminds us: "The Lord upholds all those who fall and lifts up all who are bowed down" (Ps. 145:14;NIV).

Failing is not the end of the world. It just means it is time to head in a new direction. You can fail, but you can also start again. Proverbs tells us, "For though a righteous man falls seven times, HE RISES AGAIN..." (Prov. 24:16;NIV).

3. You will not be considered attractive all the time.

Some people will even be put off by your physical appearance or your personality. Remember this one thing, you are attractive to the degree that you are yourself. Be true to yourself and don't worry about what other people think of you. God wants you to be free to be yourself.

If you do not feel attractive, have hope and start again. Above all, have confidence in the Lord Jesus Christ. Do not be afraid or dismayed.

This book is intended to communicate a wonderful truth. Every human being has received an extraordinary potential from God, even though this potential is not often used to its maximum. Although there are barriers preventing its full utilization, there is also hope. The barriers can be taken down and your potential can be achieved.

To be successful in this, it is essential to rediscover that being human is not something that happened by accident. Every human being is a creation of God and has infinite potential.

Many people believe the widespread myth "I am what I am and what I become is somehow predetermined." This is a lie because **we can change.** We were not created as machines that function in a particular way through various manipulations.

The cry of humanity is, "Help me to change."

When it seems for the time being that everything is lost, remember the best is yet to come. Hope in the Lord.

God wants to help you change the course of your life.

Yes, it is possible to have a fresh start.

Dr. Mario Rivera Mendez

Recommendations

1. Read a chapter of the Gospel of John every day, and after reading ask, "Who is Jesus Christ?"

2. Listen to the *Mental Hygiene* tapes.

3. Join a church fellowship where the Lord Jesus Christ is preached as the one and only all-sufficient Saviour.

Details of **Theotherapy Seminars,** books, and tapes are available from:

Theotherapy Seminars, Inc.
1105 Lomand Drive
Pittsburgh, PA 15235

Evangelistic Mission to Puerto Rico
P.O. Box 1537
Haines City, FL 33845

Theotherapy Seminars
8 Charles Avenue
Chechester, W.
Sussex, England P.0194EY